The Life and Times ~of the~ APPLE

Charles Micucci

ORCHARD BOOKS • NEW YORK

For little apple eaters, who ask lots of questions

Orchard Books
95 Madison Avenue, New York, NY 10016

Manufactured in the United States of America
Printed by General Offset Company, Inc.
Bound by Horowitz/Rae
Book design by Alice Lee Groton
10 9 8 7 6 5 4 3 2

The text of this book is set in 15.5 point Cheltenham Light.
The illustrations are watercolor and pencil reproduced in full color.

Library of Congress Cataloging-in-Publication Data
Micucci, Charles.
  The Life and times of the apple / by Charles Micucci.
    p. cm.
  Summary: Presents a variety of facts about apples,
including how they grow, crossbreeding and grafting techniques,
harvesting practices, and the uses, varieties,
and history of this popular fruit.
ISBN 0-531-05939-1. — ISBN 0-531-08539-2
1. Apple—Juvenile literature. [1. Apple.] I. Title.
SB363.M45 1992   634'.11—dc20   90-22779

Contents

The Life of an Apple

The apple is one of the most popular fruit trees in the world. Apple trees grow on every continent except Antarctica. In the United States alone, there are an estimated thirty million apple trees.

An apple tree may grow to be forty feet high and live for over a hundred years. But it always begins with one small seed.

Most apple cores have ten seeds. Usually, two seeds lie in each of the core's five chambers.

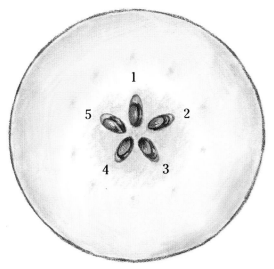

*horizontal cross section
of an apple*

Even though an apple seed is only ¼ inch long and weighs less than ¹⁄₁₀₀th of an ounce, it could grow to be as tall as a four story building.

Fruits that have seeds in a core are called pomes. Apples and pears are pomes.

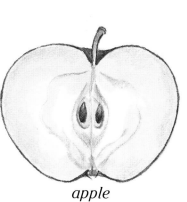
apple

pear

Apples are a member of the rose family. So are pears, peaches, plums, and cherries.

5

Planting Apple Seeds

If you planted a seed from a big, red, juicy apple, a tree might grow, and it might bear fruit. But an apple from that tree would be different from your original apple. It probably wouldn't be as big, red, or juicy, and probably wouldn't taste as good. Why?

Apples reproduce through a process called cross-fertilization. The pollen from one apple blossom fertilizes another apple blossom. This fertilized flower then turns into an apple that will produce seeds with characteristics of both parent apples. Even though your apple is big, red, and juicy, its seeds might develop into trees bearing green or yellow apples of any size or shape.

Cross-fertilization of apples

If you plant the seed from a big, juicy apple and it grows into a tree, what kind of apple will it bear?

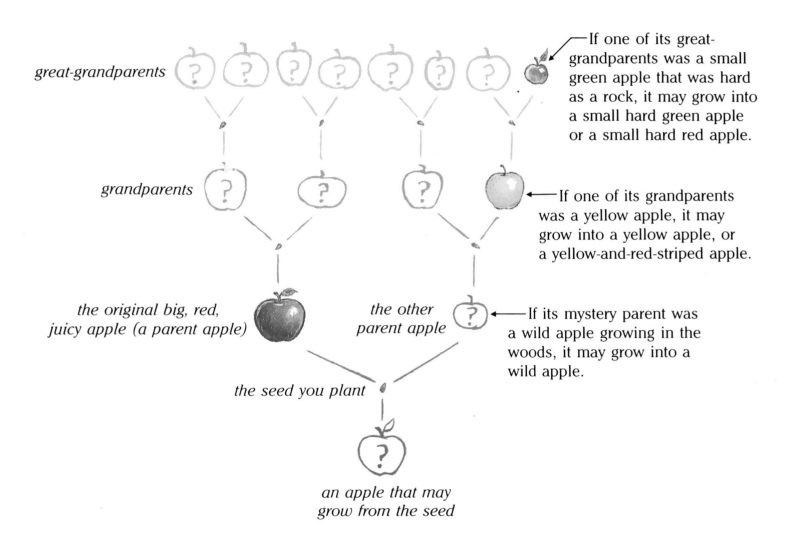

great-grandparents

If one of its great-grandparents was a small green apple that was hard as a rock, it may grow into a small hard green apple or a small hard red apple.

grandparents

If one of its grandparents was a yellow apple, it may grow into a yellow apple, or a yellow-and-red-striped apple.

the original big, red, juicy apple (a parent apple)

the other parent apple

If its mystery parent was a wild apple growing in the woods, it may grow into a wild apple.

the seed you plant

an apple that may grow from the seed

With so many question marks in an apple's family tree, you would never be able to predict what kind of apple would grow from the seed of a big, red, juicy apple.

Grafting

Most apple growers want to be able to predict what type of apple they are growing. Instead of growing trees from seeds, they use a procedure called grafting.

Grafting allows apple growers to control the type of apple they raise. The most common methods of grafting are the *cleft graft* and the *bud graft*.

The cleft graft is used by many commercial growers. On a tree that is cleft grafted, all the apples will be the same.

The bud graft is used mostly by gardeners, and to convert wild apple trees into domestic apple trees. On the branch that grows from a bud graft, all the apples will be the same. So a creative gardener could grow a tree with many kinds of apples by bud grafting different kinds of apple buds onto it.

A cleft graft joins a scion (a tree branch) to a rootstock (a tree trunk with roots).

SCION

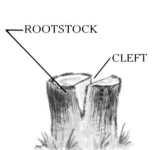

ROOTSTOCK

CLEFT

WAX

The end of the scion is cut at an angle.

A cleft is cut into the rootstock and wedged open.

The scion is inserted into the rootstock.

Wax is poured over the cleft to protect it from weather and insects.

A bud graft joins a bud (also known as a scion) to a rootstock or to another branch.

BUD (SCION)

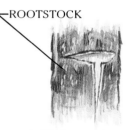

ROOTSTOCK

A bud is cut from a tree.

A T-shaped cut is made in the bark of a rootstock.

The bud is placed inside the T-shaped cut.

The bud and rootstock are wrapped with tape for support.

From these scions, a new apple tree will grow. In both types of grafting the scion determines what type of apples the tree will produce. For example, if the scion is from a Granny Smith apple tree, then all the apples will be Granny Smith apples.

Apple Blossom Time

Three to five years after grafting, an apple tree is ready to bear apples. In the summer tiny buds form on the branches. During the autumn, the buds develop and grow a covering of hair. The fuzzy hair protects the buds from ice and snow while the buds lie dormant during the winter months.

In the spring leaves sprout from the buds. Soon leaves fill the tree and little flower buds appear. Finally, as the days grow warm, the buds blossom into pink flowers.

apple buds in winter

apple buds in spring

It is important for apple buds to rest during the winter. That is why apple trees grow better in climates where winter temperatures drop below 45°F.

Apples can grow in colder climates than other fruit trees because they bloom later in the spring, minimizing damage to buds by frost.

FRUITS	BLOOM IN
CHERRIES	MARCH—APRIL
PEACHES	APRIL
APPLES	MAY

apple tree in bloom   *cherry tree in bloom*

Apple blossoms don't open until after leaves appear on the tree. On other fruit trees, such as the cherry tree, the flowers appear before the leaves.

Most apple flowers are pink when they first blossom and gradually fade to white as they grow older.

Apple blossoms bloom in groups. Each group has five blossoms.

Parts of an Apple Flower

When you look at an apple flower, you see five pinkish white *petals* that extend from five green *sepals*.
If you cut an apple flower in half, you would see much more.

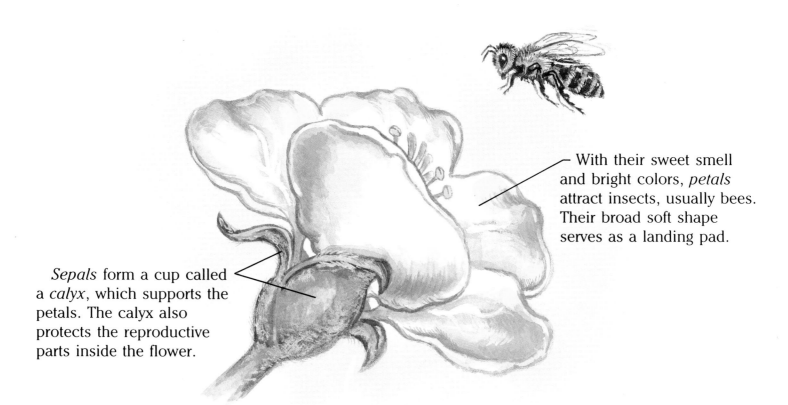

With their sweet smell and bright colors, *petals* attract insects, usually bees. Their broad soft shape serves as a landing pad.

Sepals form a cup called a *calyx*, which supports the petals. The calyx also protects the reproductive parts inside the flower.

The *pistil*, the female part of the flower, sits in the middle of the flower. The pistil includes the stigmas, styles, and the ovary.

Five *stigmas*, special sticky surfaces where pollen collects, are at the top of the pistil.

Each *style* is attached to one stigma, holding it out of the flower so insects can brush against it.

Nectar, a sweet liquid that attracts bees, is found in the center of the flower between the styles.

An *ovary* rests at the base of the pistil. It is split into five sections.

Each section, called a *carpel*, contains two ovules.

Ovules are unfertilized apple seeds.

The *receptacle* is at the base of the flower where it meets the stem.

Surrounding the pistil are many *stamens*. The male part of the flower, each stamen has a filament and an anther.

Anthers produce an important yellow powder called pollen.

The *filament* is a tube that supports the anther.

When *pollen* from the anthers of one apple blossom is transferred to the stigmas of another apple blossom, the ovules become fertilized and an apple begins to grow. This is called pollination. But apple flowers can't pollinate themselves. They need a helper—the honeybee.

Flight of the Honeybee

Honeybees, attracted by the smell and color of apple blossoms, fly from flower to flower searching for nectar, which they collect and make into honey, and pollen, which they make into bee bread.

Their only purpose is to feed themselves and their fellow bees. But in their travels some of the pollen they gather from one apple blossom accidentally brushes against the stigmas of another blossom. That's how bees help pollinate apple flowers.

When about one-fourth of the apple trees are blooming, a commercial apple grower hires a beekeeper who may bring in over a million bees to pollinate the orchard.

Honeybees do a special dance to let other bees know where they have found nectar and pollen.

Bee bread is a food mixed from honey and pollen that adult bees feed to three-day-old larvae, or baby bees.

How a bee pollinates an apple flower

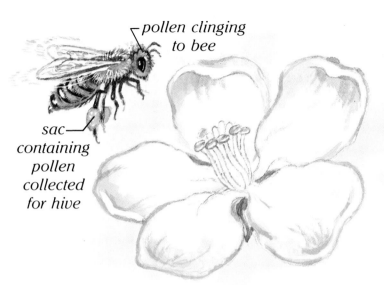

pollen clinging to bee

sac containing pollen collected for hive

A bee approaches a flower with pollen that it gathered from other flowers.

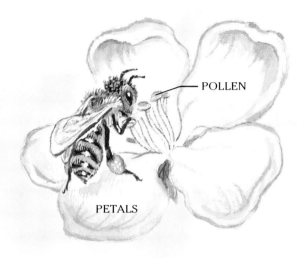

POLLEN

PETALS

The bee lands on the petals and searches for nectar and pollen.

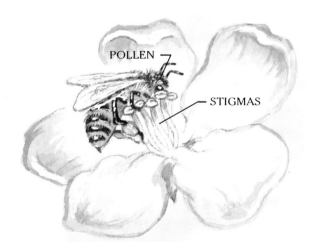

POLLEN

STIGMAS

As the bee gathers nectar, some of the pollen from other flowers accidentally brushes against this flower's stigmas.

pollen from other flowers

The bee flies away, leaving some of the other pollen behind.

From Flower to Apple

After the apple flower has been pollinated, the petals fall off, and the receptacle begins to bulge. Through the spring and summer, the little green bulge grows and changes shape until it begins to look like an apple. Toward the end of summer the apple changes color. Soon it will be ready for harvest.

Petals fall off.

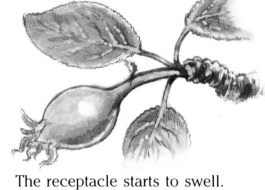

The receptacle starts to swell.

The fruit becomes rounded and begins to look like an apple.

The apple reaches full size and starts to change color.

An apple has ten ovules. At least four of them have to be fertilized for an apple to grow, but unless all ten are fertilized, it will be lopsided.

In plants, leaves produce the energy required to grow fruit. Over fifty leaves are necessary to grow one apple.

All through the growing season, apples fall off the trees. But most of them fall about six weeks after bloom (June drop), and shortly before they're ripe (preharvest drop).

Sunlight causes apples to change color by causing a chemical reaction in the sugar of apples. These reactions produce red and yellow pigments in the apple's skin.

SUN

As an apple grows, the petals fall off, but the sepals, stamens, and pistil stay. You can still see the remnants of these parts in a ripe apple.

The sepals and stamens are at the bottom of an apple.

OVARY

RECEPTACLE

OVULES

SEPALS   STAMENS

Inside an apple the pistil develops. The ovary grows into the core, and the ovules become seeds. When you eat an apple, you are actually eating the receptacle of the apple flower.

Harvesting Apples

In late summer and early autumn the apples are ripe and ready to pick. Today, in the age of spaceships, most apples are still picked just as they were in colonial times—by hand. Apple pickers, careful not to bruise the fruit, don't just yank apples off the tree. Instead, they gently cup each apple, then lift and twist it up and away from the tree. This insures that the apples will stay fresh longer and that new buds will grow on the tree next year.

The apple pickers place the apples in canvas bags they wear around their shoulders. From there, the apples are loaded into bins and shipped to market.

Apple pickers use a bag with a special bottom to hold the apples.

When the bag is full . . .

. . . they unsnap the bottom and empty the apples into a bin.

The largest quantity of apples is picked in October. That is why October is officially known as Apple Month.

Although most apples are picked by hand, some growers use mechanical pickers, which shake the fruit from the tree. Those apples are made into applesauce and juice.

Today some apple growers raise dwarf apple trees. Dwarf trees don't take up as much space as normal apple trees. A grower may be able to plant over 500 dwarf trees per acre, versus 27 per acre for some larger trees. And that means more apples at harvest.

full-size apple tree   *dwarf apple tree*

In addition to a test tasting, modern apple growers use many instruments that tell them when is the best time to pick apples.

A pressure gauge measures an apple's firmness.

A refractometer measures an apple's sugar content.

A computer calculates the climate, length of growing season, and other factors that may influence the apple's growth.

The Many Uses of the Apple

At market apples are cleaned and sorted according to type, size, and color. Ideally, only the best apples are sold fresh. Small apples, or those with imperfections such as bruises, are mashed into applesauce or pressed into apple juice. Because of their taste, nutritional qualities, and year-round availability, apples are used in more products than any other fruit.

pies

cakes

apple butter

turnovers

apple bread

caramel apples

applesauce

vinegar

in salads

juice and cider

The Pennsylvania Dutch have carved apple core dolls for hundreds of years.

Over half the apples grown are eaten fresh.

The Romans cooked apples in recipes.

About one in five apples is pressed into juice and cider.

At Halloween witches and goblins bob for apples.

Eating apples is healthy. They contain vitamins A and C, and are a good source of potassium. The pectin in apples lowers cholesterol. And eating apples regularly may help reduce tooth cavities.

How Many Apples?

Each year there are over two hundred million bushels of apples grown in the United States and over a billion bushels grown worldwide. The leading apple-producing states are Washington, New York, and Michigan. The leading apple-producing countries are the Soviet Union, the United States, France, and Germany.

Apple production is measured in bushels. There are 112 medium six-ounce apples in a bushel. One bushel of apples weighs 42 pounds.

A billion bushels grown worldwide equals about 112 billion apples. That's 22 apples for every person in the world.

Most of the apples in the U.S. grow in those areas covered in apples on the map.

The U.S. exports over six million bushels of apples, more than all the apples grown in West Virginia.

Apples are the second most valuable tree fruit crop raised in the U.S. Oranges are the first.

Leading apple-growing states

Each basket equals one million bushels of apples.

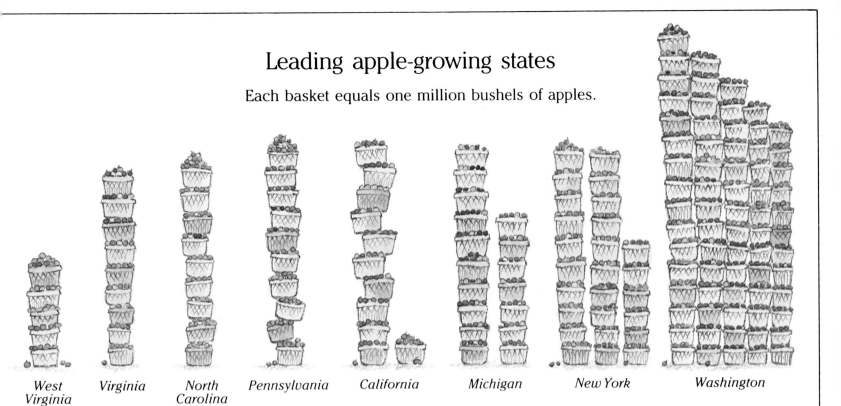

West Virginia · Virginia · North Carolina · Pennsylvania · California · Michigan · New York · Washington

Leading apple-growing countries

Each basket equals ten million bushels.

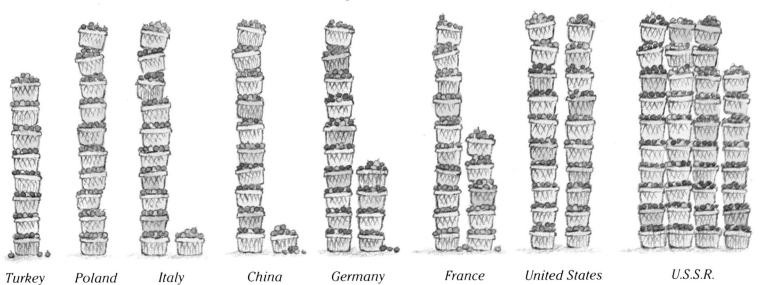

Turkey · Poland · Italy · China · Germany · France · United States · U.S.S.R.

Apple Varieties

Although there are almost 10,000 kinds of apples, only a few are raised commercially. In the United States alone, over half the apples grown are Delicious, Golden Delicious, and McIntosh.

Delicious apples total one-third of the apples raised in the U.S. Sweet and juicy, they're usually eaten fresh out of hand.

Golden Delicious apples are the most popular yellow apples in the U.S. They're good in pies or eaten fresh.

McIntosh apples are popular in the U.S. and Canada, eaten fresh or perhaps in applesauce. They serve as parent to some newer breeds such as the Cortland.

In colonial times, apples were called such fanciful names as Winter Banana, Melt-in-the-Mouth, and Westfield Seek-No-Further.

Winesap apples were grown by early pioneers for apple cider. Today they are raised in the Northwest and in the Appalachian Valley.

Gravenstein apples are thought to have originated at Castle Gravenstein, Germany (now part of Gråsten Slot, Denmark) in the 1600s. They're still grown in Europe and the U.S.

Granny Smith apples have a tart taste and are often baked into pies. They're usually grown in Australia, Chile, New Zealand, and South Africa.

Rome Beauty apples, because of their large size, may be cored, filled with raisins, and baked in the oven.

Cox's Orange Pippins are famous for their orange color. They are one of the most popular apples grown in England.

Cortland apples are used in salads because they don't turn brown as quickly as other apples do when they're sliced.

Newtown Pippins were the first apples exported from America. In 1768, some were sent to Ben Franklin while he was visiting London.

York Imperial apples have an odd, lopsided shape, as if they are leaning over.

Jonathan apples are eaten fresh, baked into pies, and processed commercially into a wide range of products.

Rhode Island Greening apples are excellent for baking in pies because they don't wilt and turn mushy when heated.

All the apples on this page are domestic apples. There are also about thirty kinds of wild apples in the world. They tend to be small and sour, but birds love them.

The Times of the Apple

Apples have been growing on earth for over two and a half million years. People of prehistoric times ate wild apples they picked from Asian forests. Later in the Stone Age, lake villagers in what is now called Switzerland started preserving apples, thus making it possible for people to eat apples all year long.

An apple time line

| 2,500,000 B.C. | 100,000 B.C. | 20,000 B.C. | 400 B.C. | 50 B.C.– |

Apples are believed to have originated in Asia, near the Caspian Sea.

Stone Age lake dwellers preserved apples by drying them in the sun.

Rome conquered Europe and took the apple as far north as England.

Prehistoric people ate wild apples that tasted bitter and were only the size of a strawberry.

The Greeks grafted apples. They had 7 varieties of domestic apples.

While apples were once grown only from seeds, in the fourth century B.C. the Greeks started grafting apple trees. When ancient Rome expanded its empire, it spread the technique of grafting across Europe, including England. As England's gardens flourished, so did the apple. It was natural that, when colonists came to America, they brought apples and apple seedlings with them.

A.D. 50   A.D. 100   Middle Ages   1307   1600s

Building on Greek techniques, Romans continued grafting apples. They had 36 domestic apple varieties.

Apples were grown throughout Europe.

Isaac Newton discovered the law of gravity while sitting beneath an apple tree.

Under threat by a tyrant, William Tell shot an apple off his son's head.

European ships sailed for America with apples on board.

In the 1800s Washington State apple growers east of the Cascade Mountains started irrigating their orchards. Today Washington is the leading apple-growing state.

In 1893 Iowa, a state known for its corn, became the birthplace of the U.S.'s most popular apple—the Delicious.

"Go West, Young Apple!"

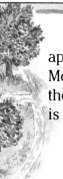

The Europeans landed in North America, many with their own apples and apple seedlings. The Dutch shipped apple seedlings to New Amsterdam, which is now New York. The French started orchards in Canada. And the British colonists planted apples, from Newfoundland to Virginia. Then, as pioneers moved west, so did the apple.

Pioneers brought apples west in covered wagons.

During the late 1600s, Franciscan priests planted orchards in New Mexico, then part of the Spanish territories.

Some Indians planted apple trees around their villages.

Apples were shipped by boats that sailed around South America.

Cowboys fed apples to their horses as a special treat.

Around 1800 John McIntosh discovered the first McIntosh apple trees in Ontario, Canada.

In 1629 the pilgrims of the Massachusetts Bay Colony received apple seedlings from England. The native crab apples were bitter, woody, chewy, and wormy.

Michigan named the Apple Blossom its State Flower in 1897.

Golden Delicious apples were born in the hills of West Virginia in 1914.

In 1730 the first apple nursery opened in Flushing, New York.

One of George Washington's hobbies was pruning his apple trees.

Thomas Jefferson experimented with several new apple varieties.

Virginia colonists grafted domestic apple branches onto wild apple tree trunks in 1647.

From 1795 to 1845 Johnny Appleseed planted apple seeds in Ohio, Indiana, Illinois, and Pennsylvania.

In 1901 Arkansas named the Apple Blossom its State Flower.

N
W E
S

In colonial America apple cider was a popular drink before there was running water.

The Legend of Johnny Appleseed

Johnny Appleseed was born September 26, 1774, in Leominster, Massachusetts. His real name was John Chapman.

While in his early twenties Johnny moved to western Pennsylvania and soon started planting apple seeds. For fifty years he planted apple seeds in the Ohio Valley. He showed pioneers and Indians how to care for apple trees; they took his knowledge westward. Today many of the apple trees in Ohio, Indiana, Illinois, and Pennsylvania are descended from trees planted by Johnny Appleseed.

Johnny walked many miles barefoot to care for his apple trees, even in winter. He fashioned a tin pot into a hat, wore an old coffee sack shirt, and carried his seeds in a leather bag.

Johnny gathered his seeds from cider mills that were spread across the country.

Johnny didn't like to sleep indoors. He preferred to be outside, under the moon and stars. His seed bag was his pillow, and leaves and twigs were his blanket.

During the War of 1812, Johnny heroically raced through midnight forests to warn settlers that they were in danger.

A missionary of the Swedenborgian Christian religion, Johnny believed it was wrong to hurt another living being. He befriended wounded animals and was a vegetarian.

31

The apple has come a long way since prehistoric times. It has earned a place in world history. But the story of the apple doesn't stop here. Each spring billions of little apple buds across the globe add new chapters to the life and times of the apple.

"An apple a day keeps the doctor away!" is an old saying based on the nutritional qualities of the apple.

The phrase "The Big Apple" was originally a slang term for Harlem, popularized by jazz musicians and poets of the 1920s. Later, during the swing era of the 1930s, it became a popular dance. Today "The Big Apple" is a nickname for New York City.

"As American as apple pie." Americans like to think of themselves as wholesome, honest, and good—qualities also found in homemade apple pie.